TROPICAL FISH

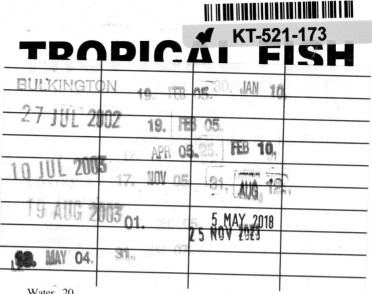

Photo by Burkhard Kahl featuring
Pterophyllum scalare altum.

The photos for the products illustrated in this book have been provided by the manufacturer. Their inclusion in this book does not imply an endorsement by the author. The products have been selected because they are nationally advertised and are widely available.

Distributed in the UNITED STATES by T.F.H. Publications, Inc., One T.F.H. Plaza, Neptune City, NJ 07753; in CANADA to the Pet Trade by H & L Pet Supplies Inc., 27 Kingston Crescent, Kitchener, Ontario N2B 2T6; Rolf C. Hagen Ltd., 3225 Sartelon Street, Montreal 382 Quebec; in CANADA to the Book Trade by Macmillan of Canada (A Division of Canada Publishing Corporation), 164 Commander Boulevard, Agincourt, Ontario M1S 3C7; in ENGLAND by T.F.H. Publications, PO Box 15, Waterlooville PO7 6BQ; in AUSTRALIA AND THE SOUTH PACIFIC by T.F.H. (Australia) Pty. Ltd., Box 149, Brookvale 2100 N.S.W., Australia; in NEW ZEALAND by Ross Haines & Son, Ltd., 82 D Elizabeth Knox Place, Panmure, Auckland, New Zealand; in the PHILIPPINES by Bio-Research, 5 Lippay Street, San Lorenzo Village, Makati, Rizal; in SOUTH AFRICA by Multipet Pty. Ltd., P.O. Box 35347, ... Africa. Published by T.F.H. Publications, Inc. Manufactured ... Publications, Inc.

BASIC EQUIPMENT

If you are planning to have a tropical fish aquarium, you are strongly advised to purchase the aquarium and its essential equipment before acquiring the fish. This is because you must create a suitable habitat for the fish to live in. You should not just place them into a newly set up aquarium that may well be a very hostile environment. Even though you may think it looks ideal, the water needs to be aged and treated. In most cases you will need a pump, a filter, a heater, and certain other pieces of equipment like a net, thermometer, fish foods, tank cover, top light and aquarium decorations like live or artificial plants and rocks. The equipment you require is based upon the kind and number of fishes that you want to keep. The need for this equipment will become apparent as you read this book. You are strongly advised to consult a large book in which thousands of fishes are illustrated and their life styles are discussed. Modern books use codes to squeeze in a lot of information into a small caption. *Dr. Axelrod's ATLAS OF FRESHWATER AQUARIUM FISHES* is the ultimate reference work of this

Everybody wants a beautiful aquarium...like this one. By following the instructions in this book, you can easily have one in your home or office.

Easily readable digital thermometers are simply pasted on the outside of the aquarium located in such a way that it reads the temperature at mid-water.

To convert between metric and English:

Length:
mm × 0.04 = in
cm × 0.4 = in
m × 3.3 = ft
m × 1.1 = yd
in × 2.54 = cm
ft × 30 = cm

Mass (Weight):
g × 0.035 = oz
kg × 2.2 = lb
oz × 28 = g
lb × 0.45 = kg

Volume:
ml × 0.03 = fl oz
L × 2.1 = pt
L × 1.06 = qt
L × 0.26 = US gal
L × 0.22 = Imp gal
cc × 16.387 = cu in
fl oz × 30 = ml
c × 0.24 = L
pt × 0.47 = L
qt × 0.95 = L
US gal × 3.8 = L
US gal × 231 = cu in
Imp gal × 4.5 = L
Imp gal × 277.42 = cu in
cu in × 0.061 = cc
cu ft × 0.028 = m²

Temperature:
°C × 1.8 + 32 = °F
°F − 32 × 0.5555 = °C

DR. AXELROD'S
ATLAS
OF
FRESHWATER
AQUARIUM
FISHES
THIRD EDITION

DR. HERBERT R.
AXELROD

DR. WARREN E.
BURGESS

NEAL PRONEK
AND
JERRY G. WALLS

MORE THAN
4,500 PHOTOS
IN
FULL COLOR!

It also provides a better viewing area when compared to round or triangular shapes, which distort the view of the fish. Ornamental shapes are fine once you have gained practical experience and can apply this experience to more unusual shapes.

SURFACE AREA: This is very important to the fish because all of the oxygen required by them is gained at this interface with the air. Not only does oxygen enter the aquarium water by the surface (unless you use an air pump, too), but the dangerous gases produced by the fishes, plants and decaying organic material, pass out of the water at the surface. Depth is important only insofar as it provides more

type. Now in its sixth edition, it has over 7,000 color photographs and is brought up to date on a regular basis.

THE AQUARIUM

Choose the largest aquarium you can afford. The smaller it is, the more rapidly it will be affected by such things as pollution from overfeeding or feeding bad foods, over-crowding and temperature variations. Select the traditional rectangular shape because this has proven to be the most practical shape to house the maximum number of fish in relation to the volume of water.

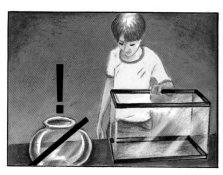

space for the fish to swim in and more room to feature decorative scenes.

VOLUME: You need to know the volume of your aquarium in order to calculate the weight of the water. Then you can establish that it will not be too great for any shelf or wooden floorboards it is standing on. It is also needed should you have occasion to add medicines to the water or have to effect a water change of, say, 10% per week.

Calculating Volume and Weight of the Water in your Aquarium

LENGTH x WIDTH x HEIGHT = VOLUME

You can calculate the volume in English or metric units. If you use centimeters, then the volume, divided by 1,000, is the volume in liters. Since 1 liter of water weighs 1 kilogram, the calculations for the volume and weight are very simple in the metric system...that's why trends are to use the metric system. An example:

An aquarium measures 45 cm x 31 cm x 31 cm. It contains 43,245 cc or 43.245 liters and weighs 43.245 kilograms.

In the American system, the volume in cubic inches is divided by 231 cubic inches to determine the capacity in American gallons. Each American gallon weighs 8.3 pounds. An example:

An aquarium measures 12 in x 12 in x 20 in. It contains 2,880 cubic inches of water or 12.5 gallons. At 8.3 pounds per gallon, the water would weigh about 104 pounds.

In the English system, the volume is measured the same way, but an English gallon contains 277 cubic inches and weighs 10 pounds. Thus the same example would be:

Don't use a round bowl for tropical fish. You shouldn't even use it for goldfish! Use a rectangular aquarium with as much surface area as possible for the space you have available.

Glass tanks are best. Your local aquarium store should have many sizes available. The larger the aquarium, the more it costs...but in the long run a larger tank is cheaper because it is easier to maintain and the fishes live longer.

An aquarium measures 12 in x 12 in x 20 inc. It contains 2,880 cubic inches of water or 10.4 Imperial (English) gallons. Each gallon weighs 10 pounds, thus the water weighs 104 pounds.

Besides an aquarium, you will also need a cover glass or full cover hood in which lighting is recessed. Other accessories are also required including plants, decorations, water changer, siphon, books, a tropical fish magazine, heater, pump and filter plus an outside readable thermometer.

MATERIALS

Glass tanks are the best. If you are commencing with a relatively small project, then modern plexiglass units are fine. They may be of molded construction, or be plates bonded with silicones. Glass units are more costly but offer advantages. They do not scratch so readily, nor yellow with age.

Some have plastic or metal frames but these are often more decorative than functional. All glass tanks are by far the best.

Hood (Canopy) and Cover Glass

A top hood is well recommended and multi-functional. It not only houses any lights to be fitted but

Aquariums have been around for hundreds of years...these drawings might have been aquariums shown in Paris in 1889. Air was pumped by hand through an air reservoir.

restricts the amount of debris that can enter the aquarium. It helps to keep heat in and prevents the fish from jumping out. A cover glass greatly reduces water loss from evaporation, as well as condensation on the light fittings. It further prevents dirt settling on the water surface. It also inhibits hands and claws from grasping the fishes.

Airpumps

Airpumps come in a number of power outputs and feature levels. Diaphragm types are now the most popular. They function by supplying air into special airstones fitted to their pipe ends. This air causes streams of bubbles to rise in the water. As the bubbles burst they create agitation to the water surface and this increases its area, thus more oxygen is able to dissolve and more carbon dioxide escapes. The current

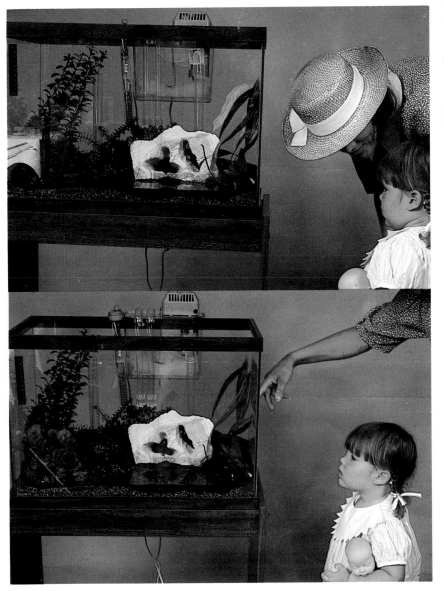

Introduce your child to the aquarium. Children will view it from a different angle than adults. They will see more of the bottom feeders than someone viewing the tank from above. Teach your child not to tap on the glass or otherwise disturb the fish. A rap on the glass might easily cause the fish to leap out of the water.

9

created by the rising bubbles also circulates the water, ensuring good aeration at all levels, and a constant temperature. Carbon monoxide and free ammonia are taken to the surface where they dissipate into the atmosphere.

Filter System

These vary in complexity and cost. The idea is that a pump draws water into a container which is filled with one or more filter media. The water is cleansed as it passes through the media and is then returned to the aquarium via a tube or by a

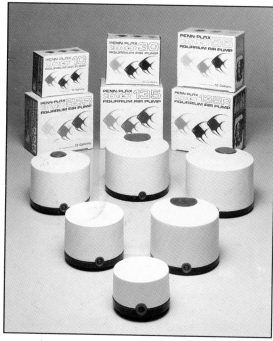

Some outside or exterior filters work on the overflow or waterfall principle.

spray bar. It agitates the water and may obviate the need for a separate aeration unit. An undergravel filter works by drawing water down through the gravel, through a filter plate and then returning up a tube to

Name	Cat.No.	For Aquariums:
Silencer 10	SL-10	up to 10 gallons
Silencer 30	SL-30	up to 30 gallons
Silencer 55	SL-55	up to 55 gallons
Silencer 55R	SL-55R	Rheostat-up to 55 gallons
Silencer 135	SL-135	up to 135 gallons
Silencer 135R	SL-135R	Rheostat-up to 135 gallons

Undergravel filters are placed into the aquarium before anything else. The filter should cover the entire bottom. This drawing shows an interior or inside filter assembled with the undergravel filter.

the surface. It encourages biological filtration, which breaks down harmful organic material into chemicals used by plants as food. In the passage of the filtered water, special filter cartridges or filter charges composed of activated charcoal are helpful in removing harmful gases and heavy metals introduced with flake foods. The charcoal is active for varying times depending on the amount of toxic material in the water.

This advertising photograph shows one of the world's leading undergravel filters in action with the gravel removed from the right-hand third of the tank in order to more clearly demonstrate how it works.

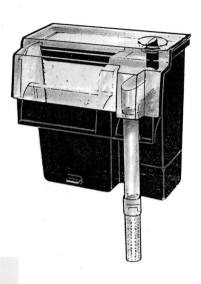

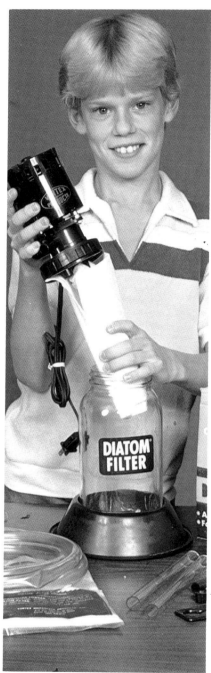

ABOVE: A typical outside filter. There are many types manufactured and sold in local aquarium stores. They are hardly a match for the canister filter, shown RIGHT, exemplified by the Diatom brand. These two types of filters cannot, however, run air-operated aquarium decorations BELOW. Such items require an air pump.

Long power cord.

Control light.

Sturdy, plastic clip-on heater holders.

Low water level cut-off.

Thick, thermal-resistant glass.

Heater & Thermostat

Tropical fish require that the water does not drop below a given temperature. (The optimum temperature varies according to species). A heater thus protects the minimum temperature of the water by heating it to the desired level. It then cuts out. Good heaters will detect even small drops and maintain the water at a constant heat. In large tanks it is better to have two heaters rather than one more powerful unit. Thermostats may be built in with the heater, or be separate units.

Thermometer

These may be free floating, fixed to the inside of the tank or to the outside. They may be alcohol, mercury or liquid crystal in method of operation. Stick on strip types are also available. You should have two

It's OK to attach your heater to the aquarium when first setting up, but connect neither the heater nor any other electrical device, while the aquarium has not been filled with water.

Some excellent heaters have digital readouts of the thermostat settings.

Digital thermometers are available for attachment to the outside of the aquarium.

Right:
The tops of heaters should have safety caps if they are not waterproof.

Below:
Most heaters are available in different wattages for different capacity aquariums.

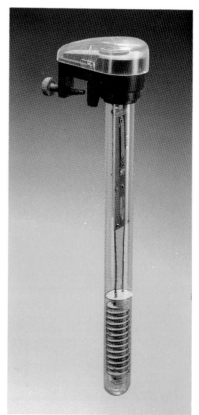

so that you can monitor the temperature at opposite ends of the aquarium.

Lighting

The modern aquarium will feature fluorescent lighting, which is economical to operate and efficient. There are many specialized fluorescent tubes to produce given effects such as plant growth and that to equate natural sunshine. Tungsten bulbs can be used but are not cost efficient. Specialized lighting, such as sodium, mercury vapor, and metal halide can be used to illuminate deep tanks not fitted with canopies.

If your aquarium hood has built-in lighting, it probably has fluorescent strip lighting. While fluorescent strips have many advantages, they did not have the intensity or spectrum of color which make the fishes look good and the plants grow. That problem has now been solved with specialized aquarium strip lamps.

Each lamp has its own characteristics. The Power-Glo has a wavelength of between 400nm and 750nm, with its greatest output in the yellow and blue range. This makes the plants grow and the fish look bluer and greener. Other lamps have other characteristics.

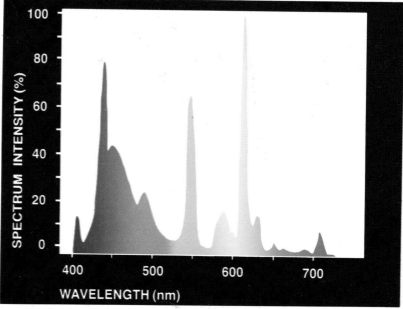

This community tank features angelfish, hatchetfish and Bleeding Heart Tetras. It is uniformly lit with light of just enough intensity to show off the fish and enable the plants to thrive without excess algae forming. Photo by Burkhard Kahl.

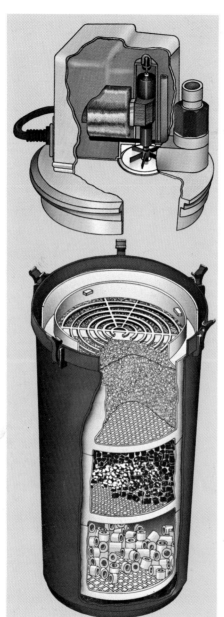

A cross-section through a high quality canister pump. The motor is on the top. To the motor an impeller is attached. The critical point is how the impeller spins while the motor is watertight. Various levels of filtration may be accomplished by using special filtering media in the filtering compartments.

Water Test Kits

In order that you are sure that the water quality is suitable to support the fishes you plan to include, you should invest in test kits for pH, nitrite, nitrate, ammonia and water hardness.

Combined or individual compound kits are available from your pet or aquatic dealer and are simple to use.

Aquarium Furnishings

The extent and type of furnishings are a matter of personal taste but would normally include the following: Gravel of one or more sizes, rocks and driftwood, ornaments, plants (real or artificial), plant containers and panel murals.

Other Useful Items

You will find it beneficial to have the following items, though they are not essential: One or more nets, algae scrapers to clean the glass, planting sticks, plant foods, gravel cleaner (siphon type), hand lens and a small spare aquarium that can be used as a quarantine/hospital unit.

The Eheim fish feeder dispenses a previously determined amount of food at a regular predetermined time of the day or night.

No aquarist should be without a water changer. It attaches to your sink from which it gets its water and discharges the used water.

The
AUTOMATIC AQUARIUM
WATER CHANGER

BETTER THAN ANY FILTERING METHOD!

Ready to use--installs in seconds

AUTOMATIC
WATER CHANGER

- No electricity
- No moving parts
- Works on any size tank
- Promotes breeding and growth
- Keeps tank clean and clear

GREATEST INNOVATION SINCE THE GLASS AQUARIUM

The
AUTOMATIC AQUARIUM
WATER CHANGER

THE WATER AS AN ENVIRONMENT

In order that your tropical fish can live comfortably in the confines of what is a very small volume of water (even in a large aquarium), it is important to understand a few basic facts about the water environment. Fish have evolved to live in certain types of water which has very definite properties. These properties are the temperature, the level of acidity or alkalinity, the hardness or softness of the water, the oxygen content, the relative speed at which the water moves, the toxic heavy metals it contains, and the amount of daylight it receives.

Clearly, a fish from the slow moving, warm, murky waters of the Amazon tributaries would not be happy in clear, cold, fast moving mountain streams. You must select your fish based on the water conditions they prefer, then provide these as near as is possible. Some fish are much less tolerant of changes than others, but those discussed in this book are not especially

This aquarium was entered into a local community tank competition in which the author was the judge and photographer. I was amazed that the water was crystal clear, yet had been taken directly from the tap! Actually it had been heavily filtered and was taken from the tap at the proper temperature. Chlorine removal tablets were also added.

demanding and will be suited to a community aquarium. Once you are experienced at maintaining water quality, you can consider those aquarium fishes with a more specific water environment.

WATER TEMPERATURE

Whilst there are numerous ways to heat your aquarium, such as by space heating (the room is heated to the desired temperature), by pad heating (the tank is placed on an electrically heated pad), by undergravel heaters, or filter heaters, the average hobbyist will use one of the various immersion heaters. These are practical and economical, both to purchase and operate. The main factors to be considered are:

1. In a large aquarium, say over 40 gallons, it is better to use two heaters in order to maintain the temperature rather

Some hobbyists use a single thermostat to run a dozen heaters...if the thermostat fails, the entire collection can be wiped out. It's better to use a separate heater/thermostat in each tank as is shown here. Photo by R. Hal Holden.

than one large one. If one stops working, the other will maintain the heat sufficiently until you replace the broken one.

2. If you use one powerful unit then if the thermostat fails you will get either no heat or too much.

3. If you obtain a heater with a separate thermostat this will enable you to place each at opposite ends of the aquarium. A more even distribution of heat will then result. This will not be a major factor in small units or those fitted with good filtration systems that ensure a good water circulation. Most heaters, however, come fitted with a built-in thermostat which, though most economical, has its drawbacks.

4. Do not purchase a heater that is barely able to maintain the required temperature, as it will be overworked.

Conversely, one that is too powerful will be switching on and off too often, which is just as undesirable.

5. The heater must be able to cope with the differential between the room temperature and that required in the aquarium. In a heated room this will obviously be much less than in a unheated room — especially during the colder months.

6. The larger the aquarium, the longer it will maintain its heat in the event of a heater malfunction or a power cut.

7. If the aquarium is well insulated it will hold the heat better, thus reduce your heater

The larger the aquarium, the longer it will hold heat. This is especially true in an unheated room. By insetting the tank into a wall, the transient temperature of the room is moderated. Photo by Jaroslav Elias.

running cost. You can stand it on polystyrene and insulate the back and side panels with cork or expanded polyurethane which is painted. This makes an interesting backdrop for the plants.

8. Fish will suffer if there is a drop in heat of more than 3°F. over a 12-hour period.

9. The warmer the water, the less oxygen it will hold, so be sure you do not overstock the aquarium.

THE pH FACTOR

The state of acidity or alkalinity of water is measured by what is called the **pH** scale. This scale ranges from 0-14,

with 7 being known as neutral. That below 7 is acidic and that above is alkaline. A movement of one unit represents an increase of ten times the upper or lower unit. A pH of 6 is ten times more acidic than one of 7; a reading of 8 is ten times more alkaline than one of 7, and so on.

Most freshwater tropical fish then add the nectar to the aquarium water. However, with most popular fish you will not need to change the pH because the fish can adjust to your tank, providing any change from their previous aquarium is gradual. It is abruptness that adversely affects fish in most matters of environmental change.

Huge pieces of wood in an aquarium may affect the pH and color of the water unless the tannic acid has already been leached out. Photo by Burkhard Kahl.

prefer a reading of 6.5-7.5. Your tap water will probably be about 7.2 or a little over this. To increase the pH value you can place some soluble rock or similar calcareous stone in the aquarium. To decrease the pH value (make it more acidic), you can place peat moss in the filter, or in a separate container, and

WATER HARDNESS

The amount of dissolved salts (usually calcium and magnesium) in water will determine its state of hardness. If the water is too hard, it will impede soap from lathering. Temporary hardness can be removed by boiling the water; permanent hardness cannot. If you have permanently hard water, you can dilute the aquarium water when making partial water changes by adding pure (distilled) water. Your fish can adjust to a range of hardness levels and most fish will accept soft to medium hard water. Any chalk or marble rocks in the aquarium will tend to make the water harder, so granite and similar rocks are the favored choice as they do not leach out their minerals as easily. Use inert furnishings in your aquarium and this will lessen the risk of chemicals creating imbalances.

LIGHT

Light is required by fish and plants in varying amounts depending on their natural environment. It also enables you to view the fish better. However, direct sunlight in an aquarium creates problems. It may be excessive and result in heavy algal growth, it may cause wide fluctuations in the water temperature (day-night) and may induce plants to grow at an angle towards the light (and even the fish to swim at an angle!). It is better to provide lighting which can be controlled and does not heat the water.

Be sure that all decorations you put into the aquarium are insoluble. If they begin to dissolve, you could have a mess. Only use those decorations purchased through a reputable petshop. This old Grecian mug is especially made for the aquarium and comes with an aerator stone.

The duration of artificial light can be from 10-15 hours per 24-hour cycle, depending on the plants featured. Fit a dimmer unit so that the light does not come on or go off suddenly, as this can startle the fish.

Alternatively, switch off the aquarium lights an hour before you switch off the room lights. Fluorescent tubes are the most favored lighting and are fitted under the aquarium hood or canopy. There are various types of fluorescent lamps, some equating natural daylight, others favoring specific areas of the light spectrum. Some special lamps are excellent for promoting plant growth. One of each is a good combination.

Tubes come in various lengths and wattages. As a guide, you will need 10 watts of tube lighting per 30cm (12in) of aquarium length, or 2 watts per gallon of water volume.

PLANTING THE AQUARIUM

Plants serve two functions in the aquarium, one being purely esthetic and the other biological. In the biological role, they grow by utilizing potentially dangerous chemicals (to the fish) as food items. They are themselves a food source to certain fish species. Other microorganisms which live on them are also potential fish foods. In needing light for photosynthesis, they compete with unwanted algae. This helps to keep algae in check. Under illumination (whether natural or artificial) they release oxygen into the water and absorb carbon dioxide. During respiration they consume oxygen and release carbon dioxide, which is why aquariums contain less oxygen overnight than during the day.

Given the benefits of living plants, they are worth the effort. They are often as much a feature of the aquarium as are the fish. You can purchase superb artificial plants and these will look as good as the real things, but they do not have the biological advantage of the living plants. They will provide shelter for timid fish and will also serve a mild biological role as places that will be colonized

Can you believe that these are mostly artifical plants? Life-like plants were first patented by the author in 1965, but I'm not in the artificial plant business now! The plastic plants look great when some algae grows on them from excessive light.

by beneficial aerobic bacteria.
A combination of real and man-
made plants is now quite
common in many aquariums.
Plants are a very good indicator
of water conditions because if
the latter are not good it is
likely that the plants will be the
first to show negative effects.
Like the fish, plants have their
own needs in relation to the
properties of water and these

must be considered if luxuriant
growth is expected. Although
some are free floating, most will
sport roots that need to anchor
themselves in the substrate.
Many can be propagated in the
aquarium by vegetative means
(simple subdivision by
cuttings).

Initially, you are advised to
restrict your planting to just a
few hardy species. Then

experiment with others as you gain experience in maintaining the plants and in controlling the factors that most effect them: light, heat, planting density and nutrient requirements. Plant nutrients, or fertilizers, are available from your pet store in

ARRANGING PLANTS

Do not overcrowd the aquarium but concentrate on vigorous growth and good color. Add plants a few at a time and see how they affect the established ones. Some plants grow well together but others may not. Always place the taller plants towards the back and sides of the aquarium, then plant the mid-tank species.

Above: Do not overcrowd your plants. Thin them out if necessary. Left: In deep water, strong-rooted plants can be manipulated with notched chop sticks. Below: Dig a depression before transplanting, just like with terrestrial plants.

the form of tablets, liquids and various compost mixtures and substrate materials. They may be placed into little containers with the plants, or can be sandwiched between layers of gravel.

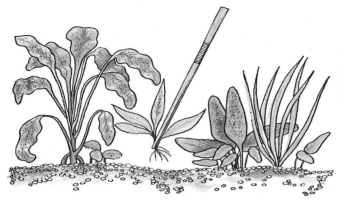

On the facing page is a Dutch aquarium...which is an aquarium set up primarily for keeping plants. Photo by Arend van den Nieuwenhuizen.

Finally, complete matters with the foreground plants. These will be short and often sport more interesting leaf shapes and colors. You will find that plantings in odd numbers are more pleasing than using even numbers. When purchasing plants, they should be well washed before being placed into your tank. Indeed, you are advised to place them in a mild saline or plant sterilization solution for about five minutes

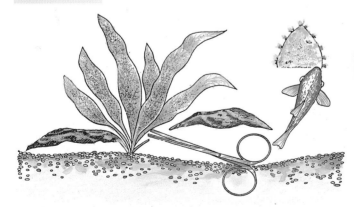

in order to cleanse them of potential parasites. Dying leaves should be removed. Once established, you must periodically thin out the plants otherwise they will become overcrowded and stunted growth will result.

ALGAE

There are many species of this group of plants and all aquarists have varying degrees of problems in controlling their growth. The green species (as opposed to the blue-green or browns) are beneficial in moderation. Your fish will browse on those clinging to rocks. Excess algae can be scraped from the tank viewing panels with a glass scraper. Mass algal growth is usually the result of too much light and not enough plantings to compete for the light and water nutrients.

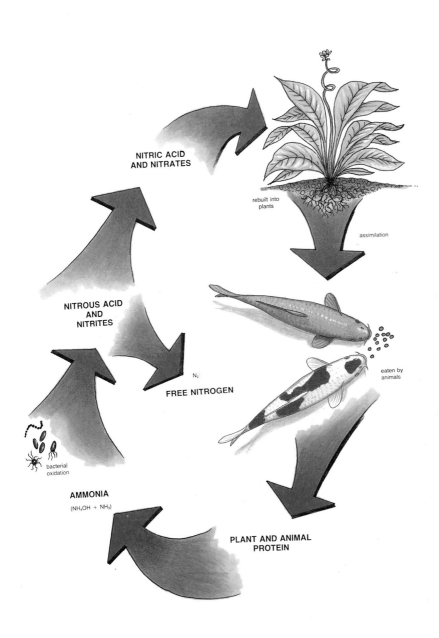

NITRIC ACID
AND NITRATES

rebuilt into
plants

assimilation

NITROUS ACID
AND
NITRITES

N_2

FREE NITROGEN

eaten by
animals

bacterial
oxidation

AMMONIA

$(NH_4OH + NH_3)$

PLANT AND ANIMAL
PROTEIN

The chemical cycle which goes on continually in your aquarium. The fish eat the food which you put into the aquarium. The food is converted into protein, with heavy toxic metals, ash and other dangerous matter being excreted or dissolved in the water. Chemically, the waste becomes ammonia. Nitrogen-fixing bacteria then convert the free ammonia into various nitrogen-based compounds which become fertilizer for the plants. The fish eat the plants or the plants grow and that completes the cycle. Only the toxic heavy metals remain to eventually poison everything in the aquarium. Most flake foods contain excessive toxic heavy metals that's why it is so necessary to change water regularly and frequently.

The best single item contributing to success in an aquarium is a strong healthy plant. The best plants are sold rooted and in small plastic pots with the roots sticking out. These are planted in the aquarium with or without the pots.

POPULAR HARDY PLANTS

There are hundreds of plant species and hybrids from which to choose, but you should commence with long-time favorites.

Vallisneria spiralis makes an excellent background plant with its tall slim leaves. *V. tortifolia* is more twisted and suits the middleground.

Egeria densa is a tall growing background plant whose leaves are arranged in whorls. Popular as an oxygenator.

The genus *Myriophyllum* contains many gorgeous species suited to the rear of the tank. Their elegant feather-like leaves need very clean water. Be sure you select those suited to the tropical aquarium as some prefer cooler waters.

Ludwigia makes a nice contrast plant because in strongly lit aquariums its leaves are red (becoming green as the light diminishes). Suited to rear or middleground, its leaves are small and quite different from those of the previous plants mentioned.

Eleocharis parvula, with its bunched grass-like appearance, looks attractive as a mid- or foreground plant.

The genus *Echinodorus* contains the many beautiful Amazon swordplants with their

Left, rear to front: *Cryptocoryne griffithii, C. cordata* and *C. nevillii.* The large plant in the center is an Amazon Swordplant, with *Hygrophila* immediately to the right and Hair Grass, *Eleocharis,* to the far right. The short, foreground plant is Microsag, *Echinodorus tenellus.*

Cuttings from Amazon Swordplants should be planted with the crown just above the gravel level.

This species of Angelfish, *Pterophyllum altum*, has never been spawned in the aquarium. All specimens are imported but they make a wonderful addition to the community aquarium.

variably shaped leaves. **Many make super specimen plants for the center of the aquarium. Be** sure you select these with care, as some are much more difficult to maintain than others — your dealer will advise you which are best. Whilst there are many attractive floating plants, these are best avoided, at least until you gain experience and maybe have a large aquarium. They can hog much of the light needed by your other plants.

SETTING UP YOUR AQUARIUM

Before attempting to set up your aquarium you should plan everything very carefully — the more so the larger the aquarium.

The site is especially important. It should be away from drafts, as these will affect its temperature retention. It should not be in direct sunlight, as this will result in heavy algal growth and also affect the water temperature, as will any nearby room heaters. If it is to be placed onto a shelf, be real sure this will withstand the weight of the aquarium when it is fully established. Aquariums full of water are deceptively heavy. A large tank on a wooden floor could present problems, so check out that the floor is strong enough. If the unit is to be placed on a stand, see that the latter is very sturdy and not likely to topple over. It will be useful if power sockets are nearby so you do not have to trail lengths of unsightly wires around the room.

This beautiful aquarium features **Tiger Barbs(***Capoeta tetrazona***)**, **Blue Gouramis** (*Trichogaster trichopterus*), **Black Mollies and Red Wag Swordtails.**

AQUASCAPING

This term relates to the way in which you design the aquarium environment and covers all aspects from the gravel to the plants, the filters to the furnishings. It is best to sketch the layout on paper so you know what it will look like once completed. Allow for plant growth. When this is done you can then place rocks, driftwood and ornaments into the dry aquarium to see how they will look. When you are satisfied, they should be removed.

Try not to make things too symmetrical but create a natural looking scene. Large rocks can be placed off center and you might have one side of the aquarium more heavily planted than the other. Keep an area towards the front of the tank relatively free for the fish to swim in, and provide some sheltered spots for the more timid species to seek refuge in should they so wish.

We all have our own ideas on what is attractive, but generally it is wise to avoid bright artificially colored gravel and excessive use of ornaments such as divers, sunken galleons and their like unless you are specifically creating a novelty tank. The natural color of plants and rocks will provide the ideal background to best display the colors of your fish without competing with them.

From the Congo River in Africa comes this beautiful Congo Tetra set against a backdrop of *Cryptocoryne* and Melon Swordplants. In the Congo these fishes are found among the heavy rushes along the banks. Therefore they feel very comfortable with dense planting. They are very peaceful. Photo by Burkhard Kahl.

Tall plants should be placed in the rear of the tank, shorter plants in front, as this sideview shows.

Undergravel filters which are terraced allow the bottom to be tapered and sloped so the debris falls to the front of the aquarium where it is easily siphoned off.

Cleaning

Once you have all you need to set up the aquarium then everything must be thoroughly washed so dust and potential pathogens are removed — this includes the aquarium. The gravel can be placed into a bucket and a hose inserted into this. The water can be allowed to overflow and you can stir the gravel until the water is quite clear. Use only gravel from pet shops as this will be free of parasite eggs or larvae, which might be found should you take this and rocks from streams. If you plan to use an undergravel filter, be sure the gravel is not too fine or this will reduce the working potential of the filter.

Setting Up

The aquarium should be on its site before you commence preparing it. If there is any risk that the site surface is not totally flat then it will be best to place the unit on a material that will cushion it — such as polystyrene, cork, or even thick cardboard. Place the undergravel filter in place if this is to be featured (but be aware it might disturb good plant growth so live plants are best placed into pots). Some gravel is then placed into the aquarium and then any rocks to be included can be gently pressed into position.

Now you can add the substrate fertilizer and then more gravel, so that there is a slope from the back of the aquarium to the front. This will look good and will encourage debris to fall towards the front of the tank where it is more easily removed. You can build terraces with rocks to help retain the gravel, or you can purchase small walls from your

aquatic dealer. Driftwood can be placed into position along with airstones (which can be hidden behind rocks). Internal filters can be sited in a

Siphon off the debris at least once a week. But when the aquarium grows thick with plants (below), siphoning is no longer necessary.

discreetly hidden position; external box filters can be placed on the back or side panels. The heater can be sited — but be sure this and other electrical fittings are not plugged into the power supply as a faulty unit could result in your getting a nasty shock.

Place a saucer onto the gravel, or some cardboard, and then you can pour water onto this. By this method you will not disturb the gravel substrate. Fill the aquarium to about half

full, at which point you can place plants into position. With water in the aquarium their leaves will float and this will make planting easier. If a suction thermometer is used, this can now be stuck to one of the glass panels. With everything on site you can then

fill the aquarium to within about two inches of the top. Add a water conditioner from your dealer to the aquarium.

The aquarium cover glass and canopy are now placed into position and the electrical equipment can be plugged in so it receives power. The heater will either be a preset model, one with an adjuster knob on it, or it will be controlled by a thermostat that you can set. It will take a variable time for the aquarium to reach the desired temperature depending on its volume, heater capacity, and the temperature differential.

Assuming all is running well, then you should test for pH value, hardness, nitrite levels and so on. The aquarium is then best left for at least a week (and up to three weeks for larger units) so you can be satisfied the water conditions are suited to the fish to be included. You can purchase a biological starter culture to speed up beneficial bacterial colonization. Once the plants are established and the water quality remains steady at the desired level, you can then introduce two or three inexpensive fish. If these prosper, you can add a few more every other week.

44

FEEDING TROPICAL FISH

Feeding your tropical fish is real easy because proprietary foods are available in an extensive range and are of high nutritious content. There is neither a need to go out searching for live foods, nor attempting to grow your own live foods. If you do decide to grow your own, your local pet or aquatic dealer can even provide starter cultures. However, there are a few basic facts that you should understand about the feeding habits of fish:

HOW FISH EAT

This heading covers two aspects of fish behavior. One is in the makeup of their diet, and the other relates to the depth of the water at which they prefer to eat. Fish can be wholly carnivorous, omnivorous, or herbivorous. You will not want to keep carnivorous fishes in a community aquarium because these are predatory fish that will eat other fish. They are not a good choice for the novice owner. Some carnivores can be trained to eat non-living things, but it is not a task for the beginner.

The omnivores are those fish that eat food of both animal and vegetable origins. The animal part of their diet will comprise small invertebrates (worms, insects and such), as well as the flesh of other animals. The flesh may simply be pieces of meat you have chopped into tiny pieces — or it could be living fish. However, they will only eat fish which are much smaller than themselves and which can virtually be swallowed whole. Providing you select them with consideration to their size, then omnivorous feeding types can safely be kept in a community environment.

Herbivorous fish eat only vegetable matter, though they may well enjoy some bits of meat or insects. In this book we are only concerned with fish that will happily co-habit with other species, though all fish will quarrel from time to time and maybe do some fin nipping, especially if they are overcrowded and territories overlap.

Fish may be surface, midwater or bottom feeders; the position of their mouths will indicate which they are. Those that eat at the surface have upturned mouths.

Use a feeding ring to prevent the floating pellets or flakes from spreading all over the surface of the aquarium. Pellets are much better as a fish food and you get a lot more for your money. Compare prices and weights. Buy fishfoods manufactured by different manufacturers so the basic formulations are different, thus giving your fishes a more balanced and varied diet.

Midwater feeders have mouths which open in the center, whilst bottom feeders have down-turned (inferior) mouths. Fish food manufacturers prepare their products for each type. There are fast, medium and slow sinking flakes, tablets and pellets, so you should purchase according to the needs of your fish and select species that represent a mix of feeder types so they are not all competing at the same water depth.

The depth at which fishes feed is relative. A fish which feeds from the mid-water areas, does so at about 18" depth in a 36" deep tank or at 9" depth in an 18" deep tank.

HOW MUCH TO FEED

Most beginners overfeed their fish. This results in pollution of the aquarium because the uneaten food sinks to the bottom and decays. Feed only what your fish consume in 3-4 minutes; always watch your fish eat, as only in this way can you be sure they all receive a ration. Any that show no interest in their food may be ill. Non predatory fish prefer a little but often, rather than have one or two large meals, which their systems were not evolved to cope with. Healthy fish can survive quite well for a week or more if you go on vacation — if friends feed the fish whilst you are away, impress upon them the dangers of overfeeding.

Apart from branded foods, which will form the basis of their diet, you can give your fish finely minced up pieces of meat, cheese, egg yolk, fishmeal, brown bread and most vegetables.

Small earthworms and other non-water animals can also be given but gathering live foods from ponds and streams is not recommended — they may harbor diseases or parasites.

KEEPING YOUR FISH HEALTHY

The potential number of ailments and diseases your fish could suffer from is legion. However, in the vast majority of cases the fish will only become ill if you are lax on one or more points of care. Prevention should be your priority. If you know how problems arise, you can then take steps to avoid their occurrence.

Most fish diseases are easily treated and there are many excellent books on the recognition, treatment and cure of fish diseases. But, if you maintain the proper pH, water temperature and don't overcrowd, you should have very little problem with sick fishes.

PREVENTATIVE CARE

The following are the main reasons for illnesses and how you can overcome them.

1. **Fluctuating environmental conditions**.

When the water temperature, the pH, the relative hardness and the ammonia levels in a body of water change rapidly, the fish are unable to adjust to them. They become stressed and are left open to pathogenic (disease causing) attack. By ensuring that the water conditions remain as correct as possible, you place no strain on the fish and they are able to develop a strong defense system against potential pathogens. You should check the conditions each week and the temperature every day.

Constant observation and study is necessary to keep your fish healthy. As with all diseases, human diseases included, the earlier you start treating a disease, the better your chances are of curing it.

2. Quarantine all new fish and plants.

Once your aquarium is established, you should view all additions to it with suspicion. Obtain a small spare tank in which additional fish are placed for a period of about 21 days. Even if the fish were purchased or obtained from a good source, they just might be harboring a disease that may show itself during this observation period. This tank should be unfurnished other than for a small foam filter, a heater, an airline, and also one or two plastic plants to provide a sense of security to the new arrivals. Slowly adjust the fish to the conditions they will find in your main aquarium (temperature, pH, etc).

Examine them carefully with a hand lens for signs of lesions or parasites clinging to their skin. Wash all added plants and see they are establishing themselves before they are placed in the main aquarium. Wash and sterilize all rocks, gravel and furnishings before adding them to your stock tank. Avoid gathering plants or food from natural bodies of water — they may carry the larvae or eggs of parasites which you do not notice. The wounds parasites create provide the openings for pathogenic bacteria to enter the blood system and thence migrate to the various bodily organs in which they live. Eggs swallowed by your fish might hatch out and so disease colonies may be created. Of course these are bold generalizations, but they do occur.

3. Remove any fish showing signs of an illness.

Such symptoms are behavioral and physical. The former include listlessness, disinterest in food, hiding away for longer than normal periods, swimming on their sides, dashing about the water for no apparent reason, and rubbing themselves against rocks or furnishings.

Physical symptoms include raised scales, a bloated appearance (other than that caused by eggs in the breeding female), skin abrasions, parasites clinging to their scales, furry looking growths, bald patches, fins rotting and cloudiness of the scales or eyes. Fish that seem to be gasping for air with their gills constantly open, or which lay on the substrate with fins extended, invariably have a problem — especially if you can see spots or blood on the gills, or if they have changed color from that which is normal to them.

In any of these instances, place the fish in a quarantine tank and carefully observe the rest of the fish whilst the patient is being treated. You may need to treat the main aquarium as a precaution. Discuss the problem with your aquarum dealer or a hobbyist who has more knowledge than you.

TREATING ILLNESS

It is only possible to treat an ailing fish after a correct diagnosis has been made. Observe all of the aquarium conditions and commit these to notes. Write down all of the symptoms, behavioral and clinical, and note precisely how your fish are fed. Also note how rapidly the condition of the fish has deteriorated and if any others are affected, or have recently died. Take this information to your local aquatic dealer and he or she will probably be able to tell you what the problem is and how best to go about treatment. It will also be worthwhile purchasing a small book on fish

diseases, or they will alternatively be found cataloged in larger volumes on tropical fish. If a treatment does not bring about a recovery in the time the manufacturer suggests,

then it is likely an incorrect diagnosis has been made, or other factors are negating the treatment. If you have a local vet that is well versed on fish matters, then do consult him or her so that prescription drugs might be used, though often prescription drugs are sold in petshops without prescriptions!

Generally, if treatment is not rapid, the fish will die, but you still should always try to save the fish.

Two Tiger Barbs, *Capoeta tetrazona.* **The healthy fish has its fins outstretched and it LOOKS healthy. The sick fish has clamped fins, its mucus covering might be cloudy, as might its eyes, it may have white spots or fungus patches on its body...and it looks sick.**

POPULAR TROPICAL FISHES

In this final chapter, a few of the most popular aquarium fish are mentioned. They represent a selection of species that frequent the differing depths of the water, thus reducing the risk of over-competition for food at a single level. However, do appreciate that surface feeders will also take food from lower levels and vice versa. The selection discussed includes a range of differing body and fin shapes, also many that are highly colorful. Some are viviparous, meaning that they give birth to live offspring, others are oviparous (egglayers). You should not breed fish in a community aquarium because few if any babies would survive. Most livebearers will readily devour their own offspring, whilst most egglayers will do likewise with the eggs they spawn. If you wish to breed your fish they must be given separate accommodations where you can control matters and protect the offspring via breeding traps or nets. Many of the fish in this chapter will breed without too much difficulty but you should gain experience before thinking in terms of propagating more fish as this will necessitate investing in small breeding tanks and the accessories that go with them, like pumps,

Angelfish and cardinal tetras, *Paracheirodon axelrodi*, get along well in this community aquarium. Photo by Burkhard Kahl.

heaters, filters and the like.

Many species of fish form schools but you may not be aware of this fact in all cases because the area required for

TOP FEEDERS

THE GUPPY, *Poecilia reticulata*

T= 18-28°C (about room

schooling may be larger than your aquarium, so the fish appear not to be in any particular formation. Do remember to select fish of comparable size so there is no risk the largest could swallow the smallest. Finally, because the fish here are grouped according to their preferred swimming depth, they are not in any order of relationship with respect to their scientific classification.

Abbreviations:
  T = Water Temperature
  L = Average Length
  B = Breeding Type

temperature.
  L= Up to 6 cm (2.5 inches), females larger
  B = Livebearer

This tiny fish is available in a multitude of colors and fin shapes. It is very hardy and a prolific breeder. It enjoys taking mosquito larvae from the surface, but also spends much time in the midwater level. The female is rather drab when compared to the gaudy males. Provide plenty of cover for these fish which all beginners are recommended to include in their initial collection. If you have a tank of guppies with no other fishes, and the guppies

Top and bottom, right hand column, are two Siamese Fighting fish. These are males as indicated by their long fins. There are dozens of color varieties found among the Siamese Fighters.

The three fish shown here are Guppies. The top fish is a wild male. The two lower fish are fancy varieties. More than 100 varieties of Guppies are available.

are well fed, they will probably not eat all their babies. They have living young every month.

SIAMESE FIGHTING FISH, *Betta splendens*

T = 24-30°C L = 6 cm

B = Egglayers.   Bubblenest builders

The brilliant colors and flowing fins of this species make them a favorite with aquarists. However, only one male can be kept per aquarium, otherwise vicious fighting will occur. Females are safe with each other or with a single male. Males may nip the fins of other species that have long fins but are otherwise quite peaceful. The species are examples of labyrinth fish

which are able to breathe atmospheric air — thus are able to survive in waters having a lower than normal oxygen content.

DANIOS, *Brachydanio* and *Danio* spp.

T = 18-24°C **L** = 5-10 cm
B = Egglayer

The danios are torpedo-shaped fish which are very fast moving.

You should keep a few of these together as they are very social and do best in groups. For the average aquarium, the Pearl and the Zebra danios (*B. albolineatus* and *B. rerio*) are preferred as the Giant danio (*D. malabaricus*) would require a quite large aquarium. The danios are reliable breeders.

COMMON HATCHETFISH, *Gasteropelicus sternicla*

T = 23-27°C   **L** = 6.5 cm
B = Egglayer

The unusually deep body of this species makes it an interesting addition for the aquarium. Most hatchetfish are rather difficult to keep so be sure you start with this species. They enjoy the company of

The Zebra danio, *Brachydanio rerio*.

The Giant danio, *Danio malabaricus*.

53

The Silver Hatchetfish, also known as the Common Hatchetfish, *Gasteropelecus sternicla*.

BLACK MOLLY, *Poecilia sphenops*

T = 18-28°C   **L** = 6 cm
B = Livebearer

The mollies are a very popular group of aquarium fish and the black variety is especially so. The species are gentle and basically herbivorous. They will help keep algae in check. They should receive special vegetable foods which are produced for herbivores. They do best if one spoonful of sea salt per 5 gallons are added to the water, as they are often native to estuarine rivers. The many domesticated forms will prefer the temperature toward the upper level indicated. Apart from black you can have greens,

their own kind. They are excellent jumpers, so the hood must always be in place on your aquarium. Provide plenty of cover for them as they are a gentle fish best kept with species that are peaceful. They are not very colorful but their shape and nature justify their inclusion in a community tank.

The Black Molly, *Poecilia sphenops*, with her babies. She was actually giving birth as the author took this photo.

marbled, and albinos. There are the sailfins with large dorsal fins (that of the female is much smaller), and lyretails with a large spreading caudal fin. Be aware that the mollies do not prosper well in changing conditions, so be sure things remain constant once established. Mollies are probably the most difficult of the common livebearers. You are better off with guppies, swordtails and platies.

SWORDTAILS & PLATIES, *Xiphophorus* spp

T = 20-26°C

L = Up to 7 cm

B = Livebearer

The swordtails are so named for the rapier-like extension to the tailfin. Their scientific name, which also refers to sword-bearing, refers to the gonopodium or modified anal

fin of the male (The sexual organ of the males). The group have been extensively bred so that today you have a tremendous range of colors to choose from. The bright red varieties are always very popular. Swordtails have a torpedo-shaped body whilst the platies are rather deeper in the body and have no swordtail extension on the males. Both are vegetarians but will enjoy some protein foods and both are peaceful community fish, though male swordtails do tend to quarrel with other males of

Brick red Swordtails, Xiphophorus helleri. This variety is a domesticated strain with long dorsals.

A male Blood Red Tuxedo Wagtail Platy, *Xiphophorus maculatus.* This strain was developed by Dr. Myron Gordon with whom I studied at New York University.

A female Brick Red Tuxedo Platy female.

Three Cherry Barbs, *Capoeta titteya.* The two males are obvious by their intense coloration. (Below) A pair of Black Ruby Barbs, *Puntius nigrofasciatus.*

their own kind. They are reliable breeders and the swordtail is unusual in that young females may develop male characteristics as they mature. Wild forms are various shades of green with much reduced red when compared to the beautiful domestic strains. They breed every 28 days at 74°F. If they are not densely populated and the young have some dense vegetation in which to hide, you can probably save a few from each spawning.

MIDDLE WATER SWIMMERS

BARBS, *Capoeta* and *Puntius*
  T = 20-28°C   **L** = 7.5 cm
  B = Egglayers
  Some barbs may grow to a much larger size than that indicated, but we are only speaking here of the most popular barbs. There are probably 50 different barbs. A

dozen cover the more popular aquarium species. They are hardy fish with what might be described as a typical fish shape, rather like the goldfish. They are best kept in small groups as they are extremely social fish and can become stressed if kept alone. They may also become fin nippers if devoid of their own kind. Not brightly colorful, they display delicate hues of gold, silver, red and green, according to species. A number, such as the Black

Ruby Barb, *Puntius nigrofasciatus*, and the Tiger Barb, *Capoeta tetrazona*, display vertical black bands. In other species the bands are broken or reduced to blotches or spots. They are lively fish and well recommended. The most peaceful barb is probably either the Cherry Barb, *Capoeta titteya*, or *Puntius conchonius*.

RASBORAS, *Rasbora* spp.

T = 22-28°C **L** = 7 cm
B = Egglayers

Like the barbs, goldfish and even the mighty koi, the rasboras are members of the very large family of fish known as Cyprinidae, the carp-like fishes. These fish swim in midwater, but often forage on the bottom as well. Rasboras come in many sizes but that given would cover most of the popular aquarium varieties. They are hardy, colorful and peaceful and require an omnivorous diet. Some, such as the Red-striped Rasbora, *R. pauciperforata*, are streamlined in shape, others, such as the Harlequin or just plain Rasbora, (*R. heteromorpha*), are much more deep bodied, so there is plenty of variety in the genus. Most contain one or more black

Tiger Barbs, *Capoeta tetrazona*. There are no specific sex differences, though males have redder noses and females are fatter.

The Rosy Barb, *Puntius conchonius*. This particular strain is the long-finned variety. The males are blushed while the females are normal silver.

57

are small peaceful fish that should be kept in groups. They possess an extra fin on the dorsal edge — the adipose fin which is rudimentary and is found just behind the dorsal fin. There are so many beautiful little tetras that you must visit your aquatic dealer to see many of them. Amongst the more popular are the Neon Tetra, *Paracheirodon innesi,* and the

spots, or a number of blotches on silver, silver-red, or a silver-blue background. As with the barbs, you should keep them in groups of four or more to ensure they are happy — they are schooling species. They are not the easiest of species to breed when compared with barbs or goldfish. But they are extremely peaceful and very hardy if kept in soft water.

most popular of all aquarium fishes, the Cardinal Tetra, named in honor of the author, *Paracheirodon axelrodi.* Another great tetra for the community aquarium, and also named to honor the author, is

TETRAS, Various Genera
T = 23-28°C   L = 3-6 cm
B = Egglayers

This group are species in the family called Characidae, which also contains the infamous piranha. However, most tetras

the Black Neon, *Hyphessobrycon herbertaxelrodi.* The Bleeding Heart Tetra, *Hyphessobrycon erythrostigma,* has a lovely pinkish sheen to it and a blood red blotch on its side. It is a little more feisty and grows larger. There are three or four bleeding heart tetras; none have ever been spawned in captivity and all are rather delicate for beginners.

ANGELFISH, *Pterophyllum* spp.

Although most beginners to aquarium keeping want to keep these very attractive fish, it must be stated that they are not an ideal choice initially. It is not that they are THAT difficult but simply that they cannot tolerate

The three fishes shown on this page are merely representatives of a large group of South American suckermouthed catfishes of the genus *Hypostomus* and related genera. Some grow very large. All are eaten in the Amazon area since they are extremely hardy and can be collected and shipped densely packed in little water. Boats ply the Amazon selling them live to the area people. The meat has no bones and tastes like lobster! In the aquarium they do a fine job of eating the algae from the rocks and glass. Two upper photos by Spreinat. Lower photo by Aaron Norman.

variable water conditions and temperature especially. As they get bigger, they would eat smaller species as they are carnivorous, and they grow to about 7 inches. If you have them at all, purchase only small examples and be prepared to keep a school of them all by themselves. This aspect aside they are delightful and peaceful fish available in a wide range of patterns all based around silver with black stripes and beautiful fins. Many color varieties exist, which are the result of more than 75 years of aquarium

hobbyist interest. One of the species, *Pterophyllum altum,* has never been spawned in the aquarium.

BOTTOM FEEDERS

The species most suited to the substrate water level are the catfish in their many forms. Whilst they were regarded for years purely as scavengers, they have been progressively appreciated for their own sterling qualities in more recent times. For the aquarium you should seek the smaller varieties, such as the armored dwarf catfish of the genus *Corydoras*. These species may attain up to 7 cm length so are a nice size. They like to live with others of their species, but will also do well with other small catfish and community fishes.

Callichthyid catfish, like *Corydoras*, have a flat ventral surface so they can stay close to the substrate or on rocks. They possess an adipose fin and armored bony plates rather than scales. Around their mouth they sport pairs of barbels — sensitive appendages that enable them to locate food in the gravel or sand. These barbels are like a cat's whiskers, that's why they call these fish *catfish*. Catfish are mainly nocturnal, which means you will not see much of them during the daytime. They like to find a quiet hidden spot to take refuge in. Do not assume they will prosper on the leftovers of the other fish. They must be fed with special foods for catfish, and these should be placed into the aquarium last thing at night. They do come to the surface at times and are able to breath in atmospheric air, which enables them to survive in the low oxygen content waters that are often found in their native habitats.

They are egglayers, depositing their eggs on leaves and stones. Many have interesting markings, such as the leopard corydoras, with its reticulated black markings on a silver body. Others are less striking but nonetheless are interesting fish to include in the aquarium. They will thrive in a temperature range of 22-28°C.

There are almost 50 different *Corydoras* species available from petshops. These catfish are excellent bottom feeders for the home aquarium.

YOUR FINAL SELECTION

Once you have made your selection of species it would be wise to gather more detailed information on them. Then discuss the selection with your local dealer, both in relation to the size of the aquarium you have purchased and in the choice of plants that will be suited to the fish in question.

Obtaining fish should be an exacting and interesting process that should be undertaken with care to ensure that you are totally happy with the mini-world you will create in your aquarium.

INDEX

A beautifully planted tank featuring angelfish and various tetra species, including bleeding heart tetras, *Pristella riddlei* and hatchetfish.